LENORA TURNER

Changing Your Comfort Zones

Why the Mind Builds Barriers and the Tools to Shift from Fear to Confidence in Skill and in Life. Moving from Stuck to Advanced Levels of Success.

You make the vision, then the vision makes you.

DR. DAVID YONGGI CHO

Contents

1

Introduction

I am not a psychologist or an expert, but I know what it is to be stuck. I also know how to move to higher levels in life and that it absolutely requires changing your comfort zones. You too can make the changes and choices to live in new and better comfort zones that mean better relationships, higher incomes and a whole lot more fun.

There are rational reasons why we tend to stay in our current comfort zones even when we long for something better. Once you understand what creates a comfort zone, why and how they work, you can begin to make the process work for you and navigate to where you want to live. These ten quick chapters will take you from understanding what comfort zones are and why they're so powerful, to how to shift and get comfortable in a new and better zone.

While growing up, I was a goof ball with siblings and close friends but I was very timid everywhere else. I won no awards and was never selected to stand out anywhere. Being a middle child, I was rather invisible even in a small family. Public speaking made me feel sick. I remember sitting in the audience of a high school play that stirred a deep desire to be on stage. Unfortunately, that was way out of my comfort zone. I lacked the confidence to even attempt the goal. Besides that, I wanted to be accepted by my peers and because it wasn't cool at my school to be in plays, there was no way I was going to risk the chance of being criticized. Being criticized was my comfort zone. I was used to it. I expected it and did it very often to myself. While I have a great number of things to be grateful for about how I grew up, our family had some weaknesses. The use of criticism to correct was one of them. Due to experience, I worked hard to avoid being criticized and joining the theater would certainly bring it to me. So I killed the desire. That momentarily exciting dream died the same hour it was conceived during a high school play.

Was that a sad story? Don't worry, it gets much better. I am excited to write this book for you. Like so many, I understand fear and emotional pain and all the loud arguments that can go on in our own minds to quickly destroy any hope of stepping out of one's comfort zone. From experience I've come to understand the games our mind plays and why it plays them. I've done the work to break free from many confining comfort zones and moved into much larger and exciting ones in multiple areas of life. What I've learned can help you do the same. I can also tell you confidently that it is worth the journey. You are worth the journey!

Years later, my desire to perform on stage came back. I faced the flood of tactics that tried to stop me and went from wondering how on earth people play lead roles to playing the lead role for 13 years in front of audiences of more than 1000 people per show. Over years in other careers, I traveled to dozens of cities and trained thousands of people around the US and the world. After being published in numerous magazines and interviewing top executives on multiple continents, I can tell you with certainty that everyone has comfort zones. Everyone faces fear. Everyone must overcome challenges and discouragement and do the work to become successful. Facing and changing comfort zones is a critical part of it all.

This book may not answer every question you have but it will offer you some understanding, real steps and real examples to help you make your successful journey to the places you dare to want to go!

I know you can do it because I did it and in the early years, no one expected it from me.

I believe in you. Let's get started today!

2

Where Are You and Where Do You Want To Go?

Before we practice changing a comfort zone, I want to talk more about what it is and why it is so powerful in keeping us from fulfilling important desires in life. This will empower you to step past the zone barriers and beliefs that can stop us before we even start.

I don't know where you grew up, who you grew up with, what the environment was or what the expectations were in your home, but we all started somewhere. Our environments bring many kinds of experiences, sights, sounds, touch, smells, activities, etc. We don't even remember the earliest events, but they happened. Repeated experiences, over time, are what become our comfort zones. That doesn't mean we liked all the experiences; it means we got used to them. Whether we lived in positive or negative or some combination of environments we became familiar with them and we learned how to live life in those environments. How we grow up becomes our comfort zone. Actually, we have multiple comfort zones; organizational, physical safety, emotional safety, financial provision, communication norms, expectations for ourselves and expectations of others and more.

Though our personalities do play a part of how we interpret things and how we respond to them, over time we become persuaded about who we are and a range of expectations about life. Like it or not, we become very familiar and even comfortable with the environment we are most experienced in. Our mind puts together our experiences into a blueprint for life. Once we have a blueprint, we humans are very good at recreating the environment because it feels right, and we understand how to live there.

Personally, I love to learn, and I am fascinated by famous sayings. Here are a few that relate to the risks of what can be limiting about comfort zones.

"There is a way that seems right, but the end is a dead end." Proverbs 14:12. A limiting comfort zone can feel like it is where you belong or it is what equals your worth, but feelings don't equal truth and can keep you stuck in an avoidance to change.

"As a man thinks in his heart, so is he." Proverbs 23:7. When you try and change your comfort zone you will run right into beliefs about yourself that are persuasive. Once we have become convinced of something we stop examining it and simply run the program like a piece of background software. Changing a comfort zone is more than changing the outside, it requires upgrading the software, removing the malware and fixing the bugs.

"You make the vision, then the vision makes you." Dr. David Yonggi Cho. Doctor Cho began as a very poor boy in South Korea. He believed that vision and dreams were the language of God. He became extremely

disciplined in using his imagination to achieve each new step in his life goals and became the pastor of the largest church in the world; one million members.

I don't know why you searched for this book, but you do. I don't know what you want to change or where you want to go in life, but you do. You want something more. What is it? Before moving to the next chapter, take a few minutes to write down a few things you desire to change in your life. You can change the list or add to it later but for now, list two to four things you want to be different in your life. These will be the two to four things you can focus on to take steps with, over the course of this book. Here are just a few examples: have healthy fun relationships; give confident presentations; make a six-figure income; live without anxiety; travel the world; become an engineer; build a successful business...

-
-
-
-

3

The Pros and Cons of Comfort Zones

To put it simply, a comfort zone is a zone that you are comfortable in.

That seems obvious but what does it really mean? I like word studies. Bear with me. Too often we assume what a word means and miss the helpful picture it can paint for us to gain understanding. Once we have understanding, we can change the zone. So, let me try and quickly paint a picture of a zone.

The dictionary defines zone as: An area or stretch of land (or sector) having a particular characteristic, purpose, or use, or subject to particular restrictions.

For example, you can think of an end zone in football, a strike zone in baseball or zone defense in multiple sports.

In your own life, you have zones or stretches of subconscious land (areas or experience and expectation in your mind) that serve a purpose. That zone or blueprint looks a certain way based on your experiences that became your belief system. It has characteristics, it has boundaries that may be restrictive with detailed rules. It is those boundaries and restrictive rules that set a standard for you and can keep you from exiting those boundaries for very long.

Examples of life zones: a level of self-esteem, expectations in relationships, habits of health, typical stress levels, range of financial provision, believed limits of intelligence, trained responses and attitudes, range of joy or well being.

Now what about comfort? Comfort is defined as a state of physical ease and freedom from pain, limitation or constraint.

So putting this together, a comfort zone is an area or territory in your subconscious that is at a state of ease and not limited as long as it is within its boundaries and specific characteristics that serve a purpose.

So what are you saying Lenora? What I'm saying is that after years of my own battles, failures, successes and study combined with several decades of training, coaching and observations, it is visibly obvious that our personal, internal subconscious blueprint of life, has a profound amount of control over our lives and personal results.

Once we grow up, we all function primarily within our comfort zones. We feel at ease within our mental boundaries. When those boundaries are pushed, we begin to lose comfort, we feel uneasy, and we want to get back to the zone we're comfortable within.

As mentioned above we each have numerous comfort zones. Are you in high school or do you remember high school? Did you end up hanging out with friends that somehow felt like it was where you fit in? How about within your immediate family. Did you have a reputation within your family? What was the reputation? How did you get it? Was it fair? If not, did you fight the reputation or judgment or eventually accept it? Did you consider yourself smart or not? Were you shy or not? Were you considered a troublemaker or not? Did you believe you were attractive or ugly? All of these and more, though impacted by our personality type and strong influences over time, were formed through various experiences and messages until you became persuaded and then comfortable within a zone or range of comfort.

Unfortunately, this is true whether the life experiences and messages were extremely positive, extremely negative or somewhere in between.

Long ago I attended a two-year bible school. It was a small school with students from many different backgrounds. I think we had fifty students in our first year and about 25 of us started the second year. Half of those graduated from the two-year program and we all became good friends. During the second year, on every Friday, the group sat in a circle with a group leader that had spent 25 years in prison where he became a Christian and after release he helped others get free from destructive thinking. On Friday's he met with us for a couple of hours and anyone who wanted to, talked through personal challenges or conflicts they were having. I still remember three of our basic stories that opened my eyes to the influence of different upbringings and comfort zones. One story was Mark's. One was mine. One was Carla's.

Mark said the family he grew up in had quite a mix of chaos, police chases and that everyone smoked pot. This was decades before it was legal but because of how he grew up, he thought that **everyone** grew up smoking pot. That was normal for him and everyone he was around, so this is what he expected other families to be like. He was shocked when people hadn't smoked pot before. He assumed they were joking.

I grew up in a mostly middle-class Christian family that went to church every Sunday. My four grandparents went to church. Every aunt and all but one uncle was Christian. All the cousins I knew went to a church similar to mine and believed the key bible teaching about Jesus Christ being the son of God, sent to pay for and remove all of our mistakes and wrong choices if we simply received it. Because of my experiences, until I was full grown, I thought that **everyone** knew who Jesus was and what he did. I was aware that some didn't accept what he did but I thought they at least knew his story. I was shocked when they didn't. This was my comfort zone.

As for Carla, she grew up in a family different from both Mark and me. She spoke of a home with a lot of anger and darkness. She talked about some physical abuse, and I specifically remember the day she talked about seeing ghosts. She talked about it like we all knew what she was talking about, like we all saw the same things in our homes. She thought that the way she had grown up was "normal". It had been normal for her. She was shocked when she learned that it wasn't a common experience or comfort zone for anyone else in the room.

We all learned so much during those two years, but those three examples woke me up to the different worlds we each may come from. Our three distinctly different upbringings had resulted in three very different comfort zones with different subconscious territories and boundaries to face and overcome. Thankfully we had plenty of opportunity to stretch and get comfortable in some new comfort zones. We remained friends for many years but eventually lost touch. The experience will always remind me that we each have a different "normal" or "comfort zone" that plays a powerful role in the foundations we build from.

4

The Mind Builds and Protects the Zone

This will be the last chapter with a focus on explaining comfort zones, their power and purpose. But do stick with this important piece. Personally, I think you'll come out impressed with your mind and better equipped to work with it. In the next chapter we begin the exciting steps toward new and higher zones of success and achievement.

When we are born we are born into whatever situation we land in. We are completely dependent, and we are learning machines.

I have no idea what type of other people's comfort zones you were born into, but other people's comfort zones eventually did have an impact on what became your initial comfort zones. However, this chapter is a focus on our mind's many jobs regardless of the input. While you are busy learning to eat, crawl, walk and speak…, your mind is doing a whole lot of additional work on your behalf. It is receiving, feeling, categorizing, interpreting, learning, managing, building cases, estimating, warning and protecting for a key goal of surviving.

Both your brain and mind manage a stunning number of jobs. For simplicity, let's say that the brain is focused more on the management of the body and the mind is working more on your interpretation of this new world. Part of what the mind does is store pictures, words, sounds, feelings, experiences and stories. We learn from all of these, and we begin to make judgments and interpret to ourselves what the stories mean. Over time we have quite a library stored up. That library of experiences are the stepping stones and resources for our learning. They sink into our subconscious mind and the belief system we become persuaded of will become the autopilot of the large majority of our lives.

A comfort zone is more than a mindset, it is a belief system based on persuasive experience. A comfort zone includes feeling "at home" through experience within a territory. Once a conclusion has been made and the proverbial stakes are in the ground, leaving that territory or zone is judged to be risky by the mind. Your mind and brain will likely work hard to convince you that it is not wise or worth the effort to change zones. Sure, you might step out now and then, but after all the work that has been done to get comfortable, living within the known zone is much easier. It feels safe and it feels like it is where you belong.

A comfort zone becomes like an overprotective companion. This is because change involves feeling the boundaries of our comfort zones. Feelings are powerful tools and when triggered, if not examined as to the belief or experience they're attached to, they are extremely effective at protecting the boundaries of the zone.

A comfort zone can be like a persuasive lawyer. It knows all the reasons why you have the current comfort zone and why you became convinced of your place within this zone. It understands the rules for the zone defense better than your conscious awareness and uses every trick in the mind-body play book, to keep you within that zone.

Your subconscious has become persuaded that the zones it has worked so hard to understand and function within are who you are and where you belong. As far as the mind has been trained, these zones are your lot in life. Now it is the mind's job to keep making sense of your zones, to be fruitful there and to multiply.

If you grew up in an amazing, loving and abundant environment, this is wonderful news. You already understand much of what it takes to create that world and it feels comfortable to you.

This can be challenging news if you grew up in difficult zones. It means you have some work to do but that you can make lasting changes in your life when you exchange the zones that don't and can't produce the life you want to live.

Fortunately, all this information is actually exciting news. No one has grown up in perfect environments. Everybody faces some amount of trauma and loss. Everyone gets misinformed and misinterprets some information received. Everyone gets stuck in some of their unfavorable zones. What is exciting is now that we have gained some understanding of why zones are so powerful and why we can get stuck, we can get unstuck and move out.

Remember the earlier statement by Dr. David Yonggi Cho? "You make the vision, then the vision makes you." The rest of this book is about tools for changing your vision and changing your comfort zones.

This will require effort and patience. You're going to need to make friends with yourself.

You're going to need to cooperate with yourself, ask and answer questions of yourself, encourage yourself and applaud yourself to achieve and learn to live in a new zone.

5

The Power and Boundaries of Your Zones

At the end of chapter one, I asked you what you wanted to change. Now is the time to look at that list, ask a few questions about what has stopped you from making that change so far and what steps might be needed to make lasting change.

For example, I wanted to become an actor. The desire first came to the surface in high school. It was an exciting feeling to imagine myself on stage like the people I was watching. It seemed fascinating to play a character and act out a story that made people feel something.

But as that desire began to arise out of my heart, it became immediately clear that was in direct conflict with several of my comfort zones. First, it collided with my self esteem comfort zone. It is still kind of awkward to describe something so uncomfortable and very painful at times, a comfort zone. But I think you understand what I mean and what I mean is that I had a low self-esteem but that low self-esteem had long become my normal zone of familiarity about myself...my comfort zone. My courage to step out into acting opportunities recoiled like a sea anemone at even the thought of being criticized. Being criticized was a familiar comfort zone. As expressed earlier in the book, my dream to act died the same hour it was conceived. The established self-esteem zone was convinced that this new desire was not at all a safe venture and the feelings of fear were called up. Those feelings didn't even need to tell me its stories. My autopilot shortcut did its job with perfection. With the mere sense of the fears that all the previous story conclusions brought, the zone barrier slammed down the gavel to close the case against any risk of this potential new adventure.

Second, my desire to act also collided with the boundaries of my sense of identity at that time. The rapid fire of the comfort zone's attack began before I could prepare or even consider a response. "Who do you think you are? You're not an actor. This is high school theater. It's not even real. Do you see who is on stage now? Sure, he's surprisingly good but that's Joe. Everyone knows that Joe is not cool at all. You want to be like him? You're already unimpressive. This group can't help you."

And just like that, the two comfort zones had won. At the time they were stronger. They had the experience, and I believed their conclusions. They weren't right in "protecting" me, but they were accurate at the time because I firmly believed some painful thoughts. Those beliefs stole what seemed like a bright hope for fun and joy. Maybe the new desire would have had a chance if I had shared the idea with someone that I trusted would encourage me. Unfortunately, that didn't even come to mind as the experiences in that area were too few to draw from.

Unfortunately, I never spoke of it and didn't consider it again for many years. The good news is that I did consider it again and through some efforts, brand new experiences and input, I completely conquered the old comfort zones that used to hold me back. Now those old zones have become quiet and uncomfortable. I moved out of them. For years

16

I have lived in much bigger and better zones that match the definition of comfort so much better.

In the next chapter, we'll begin to take steps to move out of our limiting comfort zones. For now, select one thing or area of your life you want to change, write it below, then answer the questions that follow. Because we run so much of our lives on auto pilot, it is important to take time to question or examine our comfort zones. It is also important to be patient and kind to yourself during this process.

Questions:

Something that I want to change is:

I want to make this change because:

The comfort zone(s) that I have right now that this change will bump or crash into are:

Regarding the comfort zone(s) I want to exit, what do you like and dislike about the zone(s)?

- Likes:

- Dislikes:

What are some of the thoughts and feelings that come up when I think about or have tried making this change so far?

- Thoughts:

- Feelings:

On a scale of 1 to 10, with ten being most afraid, how much fear do you feel right now about making this change? ____

What are the concerns that are attached to that level of feeling?

On a scale of 1 to 10, with ten being most hopeful, how hopeful do you feel right now about the possibility of making this change? ____

What thought(s) bring the feeling of hope?

What thought(s) from what you've read so far bring an increase of hope or confidence in your ability to make a change you want to make?

18

On a scale of 1 to 10, with ten being most comfortable, how comfortable do you feel right now about the idea of taking steps to make this change?

————

What or who would make you more comfortable?

Think about the example of the mind as a lawyer. Are there experiences that were used by your mind to convince you of what you are worth that will need to be re-examined? Are there judgments or verdicts about you in your mind that will need to be overturned?

Painful beliefs bring painful feelings, and they also steal energy and motivation.

Your mind may have been trying to protect you from harm by bullying you against taking a risk. That used to sound crazy to me, until I slowed down and discovered it could be true. The mind does a lot to keep us safe. Sometimes old tactics that kept us safe from previously common attacks aren't necessary anymore. Like speaking to a child, one can say shh to those old tactics, calm the mind down and explain that it's going to be okay. It is safe to come out now and try new things.

6

The Superpower of Your Imagination

When considering the power of a comfort zone, all the work that the mind does to build it from experiences and environments, it can be intimidating to consider what it may take to change one. Fortunately, there are numerous tools we can use and actions we can take to achieve success. The more you understand how things work and the more you learn how to make these things work for you, the more excited and motivated you can become as you achieve new levels of success and know why it happened.

This chapter is about one of our greatest superpowers for changing comfort zones. It is called our imagination.

We see in pictures all the time. We don't do hardly anything without using our imagination. You remember where you parked when you go to the store by storing that image in your mind. And many of us know what it is like to wander around for a while if you were too distracted when walking into the store.

We have libraries of movies in our mind. Depending on the experience that created it, we've played that movie many times, built a story around it and made a case about it.

The superpower key is to use your imagination for you; don't let it be used against you.

The imagination is profoundly powerful and useful. The imagination is where inventions come from. Think of the Wright brothers or look them up. Orville and Wilbur Wright must have had great imaginations and determination. If you're of a certain age range, you already have snippets of a black and white movie about them playing in your mind. Black and white not because of your age but because that is all that was available at the time the first flight was filmed.

Anyway, the imagination can take us off into daydreams, it can help sort out the day through dreams at night, it can inspire great ambitions and it can also shut them down. It can produce nightmares and be used to strengthen fear.

Regarding comfort zones, the key is to use your imagination to build a comfortable space for your new comfort zones. Use your imagination to imagine possibilities and to conquer risk. Then take actions toward new experiences. The stronger or more powerful the images or experience, the more helpful they are to help your mind and heart make a shift.

Here is a story to help demonstrate the large amounts of negative thoughts and images that can keep us restricted and how to use your imagination and actions to help you win against them.

Back to the theater. By the time I reached my twenties I had had some powerful experiences with God which resulted in some major shifts in my self-confidence and many other areas. By my early twenties I dabbled in writing short plays and even gathered a few friends, cast them in my show and we performed it in front of maybe 50 people at a young adult's group at a church. I turned down the opportunity to lead further efforts because after pondering the opportunity I graciously declined because I didn't want to commit that level of time and effort toward leading the work. In that case, it wasn't a comfort zone issue, it was a lack of desire and timing issue and the right decision for me. Several years later, I had the opportunity to play a small part in a large annual women's event. I was extremely nervous but excited about the opportunity. My part had three short paragraphs. We practiced on stage, I practiced in my mind, and we performed, in front of nearly 2,000 people. Out of fear, I briefly forgot one of my lines in my second two sentence paragraph, but then remembered and we got through it all.

The next morning, I woke up exhausted and glad it was over. My husband at the time had been quiet that morning and I asked why he hadn't asked how it went. He said he thought I needed rest. I agreed but said, "but you should at least ask how it went." So he did. And I proceeded to have the first ever panic attack of my life and told him I couldn't talk about it.

I was shocked at what had just happened. The event was over. Though I had had a stumble during the performance, it was a success overall. What I realized is that I had stepped so far out of my comfort zone that it triggered panic even after it was over. It was like my old comfort zone was saying, "How dare you put me at such high risk! I can't even remember it comfortably!"

In this case it was a one-time performance, so I had time to let it sink in before attempting anything similar again. I thought the post panic attack was kind of a funny story, but it taught me about the risks of stretching comfort zones too fast. Thankfully it had been an overall success, or the experience would have added to the old argument for staying in a smaller, limited but seemingly safer zone.

Within a year I got another chance to play a small and funny character part in a large spring women's show. We practiced for weeks. I practiced in my mind and on stage. It went well and I was able to enjoy it. The next year I was given a different character and small part to play and was glad that I was a part of the team. As I prepared for my part that time, I watched the lead characters and wondered, how on earth do they do that? How do they play the lead roles? How do they remember all those lines and how do they get out there and do it? What if they screwed up? I couldn't imagine it for me.

The next year I was given the lead role. The character was funny, over the top with energy and completely unaware of her ridiculous sense of fashion. It was that character in a smaller role I had played the previous year. She had become so popular that she (and I) got promoted. Now I had to imagine it. I also had to face the very real fear of doing it. Sometimes I wondered why I was willing to face what some call, 'the terror barrier'. The comfort zone border that screams inside with any tactic it can use, "YOU CAN'T DO THIS! DON'T DO THIS! WHAT IF YOU FAIL?" It uses tactics such as sweat, stomach aches, lack of appetite, increased appetite, headaches or dreams of multiple types of failure on stage, etc. It was the old comfort zone's subconscious plot to keep me safe. Safe from feeling the horrible pain from my former belief about being stupid. I didn't want to believe I was stupid but if I screwed up, I would be demonstrating what I thought being stupid was and that terrified me. It was also the wall to keep me safe from my belief in what it meant to fail in front of a very large crowd of humans. I wasn't sure what that meant but it was obviously horrible and probably meant that I was in fact, worthless. Deep down inside I was afraid I was worthless. I did not want to prove to myself that I was worthless even though I don't know when I decided that my performance determined my worth. It was an internal trap to keep me in the comfort zone that my mind and body had worked so diligently on together, to keep me away from people's criticism and negative opinions and more evidence that could convince me that I was a loser. Can you see that I had been convinced of a lot of painful beliefs? I was to avoid the risk of all the opinions and all the power I gave each of those opinions, just in case they were negative, which unfortunately, I was afraid they would be.

By the time I got the lead role, I had grown enough in experience and confidence to be comfortable enough to take the risk and accept the opportunity. The desire in me to perform was strong enough to help me face the soon to be screaming rules and barriers of the comfort zone I had at the time. For the first several years I faced intense fear when I walked out on stage on opening night. I didn't understand why it was so intense for a long time. My newly chosen future comfort zone was anything but comfortable in the beginning. On a scale of one to ten, ten being terrified and one being incredibly fun and comfortable, I started off breaking the meter at eleven (the time I had a panic attack the next morning). The next year was a 9.75, the next was a 9, the next two were about a 7, the next was maybe a 6. Around the 7th year playing a successful comedic host that the audience loved, my meter spiked back up to a 9 for a while as my mind was attacked with brand new thoughts of failure. The attack was, "THIS YEAR YOU ARE GOING TO FAIL! It is **bound** to happen! This is the year **it will!!!**"

I had to choose my imaginations and my reasoning very specifically. I thought about the odds and decided that it didn't have to happen. Plus, I was a praying girl and since God doesn't fail, with his help, I didn't have to either. I chose my thoughts over and over until the attacks became quieter and weaker. At first, I had to push those thoughts away hard. I would close my eyes and imagine using my hands to push them away. "NO! It won't happen!" I said to myself. "We will all be successful again this year." Then I would imagine the end of a successful show. I would imagine great applause and recall the feelings of success. "We did it successfully again this year!" I imagined... and in reality, we did.

For a total of 15 years, I was on the stage each spring in front of 4,000 to 5,000 people. For 14 of those years, I played that same character (different script), and for 13 of those years I played the lead role. Did I ever make mistakes? Yes, I did. My microphone quit working in the middle of a scene once, I improvised with the event host during the mic change. The crowd loved it. Once I forgot which scene I was in and had to improvise for a line or two until I remembered where I was. I stayed calm, played a little extra on stage while trusting my mind to recover and it did. The crowd never knew. The director spotted it, but even she had to ask and was pleased at the outcome.

Year after year the shows sold out. Eventually I wrote parts of the show. After 15 years the character and the event retired but I grew in so many ways from the experiences I wouldn't trade it for anything. Sometimes during the second 7 years of doing the show I got too comfortable and decided to drink extra coffee before the performance to be sure I started with enough high energy. Overall, it was an amazing season of my life. By the end I had long since lived very comfortably in a very different and much larger comfort zone that has paid off ever since in countless ways.

I wasn't a quick shifter into my new, larger comfort zone, but I'm certain it would have happened much faster if we had performed the shows for more than two weeks each year.

One of my all-time favorite comments was from a friend who texted me after a performance, "Great job. The way your character plays encourages everyone in the audience to be free."

Your journey to a higher or better comfort zone will also pay off for the rest of your life. It will be worth the work, the choices and facing the internal arguments along the way that beg you to stop.

You'll come to feel safe and comfortable again in the new zone. It just takes some time and new experience. Like me, you'll need to use your imagination to envision yourself successful in the new zone. Your mind treats the imagination like it treats reality. Using your imagination on purpose helps build experience as you construct new familiarity for a new comfort zone. You'll also need to practice shutting the door and saying "NO" to painful negative beliefs about your worth or intelligence or the harassing thoughts of failure. Especially when failure is not the end, it's just another practice day. Forgive yourself or others for failure, learn from it and then hit the delete button as many times as it takes to wipe your mental and emotional hard drive. Failure doesn't equal you, it just happened to you. Get up, ask God for help and become the miracle you were designed to be.

Questions:

How can you use your imagination for yourself in the area(s) you want to change?

Will you practice this imagination for at least five minutes per day?

Do this exercise preferably first thing in the morning, or just before going to sleep (or both). Besides using this simple exercise every day I was preparing for a theatrical show, I also tested the effect for a week once when learning the 10 keys on a numbers keyboard. Though this is a skill that is rarely used now except for accountants, I needed it at the time and it literally shocked me at how well it worked. Use it to help build a new comfort zone. Your mind will really benefit from the help this is to get your own mind on your side, for the shift.

Will you commit to shutting down negative imaginations that work against what you want?

7

Preparation and Practice

The imagination is powerful preparation and practice for new skills and leaps into new comfort zones. This chapter is about two other best friends for change. Walking and talking.

I'm going to use another example from the stage. I really didn't plan to use so many theatrical examples when writing this book, but it is tough to beat such relevant stories.

In theater you block your scenes, and you learn your lines. Blocking a scene is to determine where your character is going to be standing or what the character will be doing during the scene based on the needs and motivations found in the script.

Think about your new comfort zone goal. Is there somewhere you can go to gain familiarity with the new zone? If so, walk around the new space. Find ways to get comfortable in this new area.

For comfort zone changes you will come up against what "feels" normal. A practical example I can share is about furniture shopping. Years back I rarely thought about furniture. I rarely shopped for furniture. Until that day, I didn't realize I had a comfort zone about shopping for furniture. Somehow, I ended up inside a store called Restoration Hardware. It was like some kind of epic music began in the background of my mind while I met and fell in love with several of the elegant styles and the excellent quality. I had an epiphany about home interiors. I suddenly realized for the first time in my life, I do have a style! This is it!

What came as a surprise is that the first several times I visited a location I began to feel uncomfortable. I actually began to think that the salespeople would wonder why I was wandering around. I felt it was obvious that I couldn't afford the furniture.

My son, daughter and I were wandering around one day in the store and seven or eight different types of catalogs were laid out in small stacks in the middle of the store on a gorgeous table. They were set out for customers to take. My eyes were drunk with the beauty I saw as I flipped through the pages. I wanted to take a catalog from several of the stacks but didn't because I felt like that would be stealing. I actually **felt** like I would be stealing because I knew I couldn't afford to buy what was in the catalog. Then I felt like I should leave the store because I was only wasting the salespeople's time. They weren't doing anything to help me at the time, but I still felt like they knew if I asked for help, I would just be wasting their time. That uncomfortable feeling that was coming from being outside of my financial comfort zone, was actually becoming thoughts and feelings to usher me out the door and back into the fresh air of comfort.

It makes me laugh now to write out this story but at the time it wasn't fun. I actually felt compassion for myself once I recognized what was going on. I was not a thief, and I was not wasting anyone's time. I went back until I could take a catalog home and not feel guilty and I could look around comfortably. Later I made a goal and bought a couple of pieces of furniture from there. Now I don't care so much but it felt good to respect myself and destroy, through practice, the lying feelings and thoughts that once tried to push me out of a store.

Back to learning your lines. Learning your character's lines requires time and practice. The more the lines, the more the time and practice required.

You are the main character in your story. Start practicing talking about yourself and your new vision and comfort zone out loud. Not out loud to everyone you know. In fact, you may need to be very selective in who you share your plan with. Select a person or a few people who will encourage you.

As for yourself, talk about it out loud in the mirror, or in a journal until you are "off book". In theater this means that you have your lines fully memorized. In my example I want you to do it until you get comfortable saying it, imagining the reality of it, and can feel the normalcy of a new comfort zone.

If you aren't willing to practice, then you're likely to stay in your old comfort zone. On stage, you do what you practice. If you don't practice your blocking, you can get lost in the scene. If you don't practice smiling when you provide training or make a presentation, you'll assume that you did but your audience will most likely have experienced otherwise.

When you practice you build trust with yourself, and you increase your confidence in this new and important journey.

Imagination, preparation and practice are your best friends against fear of failure, doubts and new comfort zone jitters.

Imagine, prepare and practice for the win.

Questions:

What two things will you do to prepare and practice for your new comfort zone?

How many times a week will you intentionally take an action to help you get comfortable in your new comfort zone?

8

Choose Your Focus

Y ou're aware of what creates a comfort zone and the purpose it serves. You are also aware of some of the tactics and fears that will arise when you step out of a comfort zone.

When you are stepping into your new comfort zone it helps to choose your focus. As a corporate trainer I stood in front of many different people with many different titles and levels of responsibilities. I loved it and built an excellent reputation. In the early days, I had to work harder at my focus or I could be easily distracted. The look in people's eyes could distract my focus if I began to imagine someone's lack of attention was my fault. That imagination could trigger new thoughts and insecurities and further deteriorate my level of confidence.

The more you let your focus wander, the less secure you may feel about your decision and your abilities. Choose your focus. As a corporate trainer, a classroom focus that helped me was often to keep the purpose of my presentation at the front of my mind. How was this course going to help the listener? This focus helped me take the focus off myself, which is an inward focus, and turn my energy to an outward focus which was more empowering.

If you can describe a focus that benefits both you and those around you, do it. Being blessed and being a blessing... both are good.

Questions:

For your change or your goal, what focus do you want to keep at the front of your mind?

Why do you want to make the change you have chosen?

Describe how will you benefit from the change?

How will others benefit from the change?

9

An Audience of One... Or More

When you are actively taking steps within a new and larger comfort zone, you will feel all kinds of feelings and likely have all kinds of thoughts. Begin to observe them but don't let them control you. You have some understanding about why you are feeling and thinking these things. Become an audience for your own process. Then become an ardent fan of yourself and your new goal. When cruel thoughts come up, disagree with them. You may want to actually say that that thought is a lie. If the negative thought seems fierce, be fierce back. It is a thought, not a reality. Then state a positive and opposite sentence. Yell it if you need to. The more you practice, the weaker the old comfort zone fears and thoughts will become. Keep in mind that they will also whisper. Don't listen to those whispers. Tell them to stop talking. They are lies and they are not the boss of you. Over time you will become persuaded of new and better things. Choose to become persuaded so you can live securely in a new comfort zone.

If you have a friend that you trust, tell them about the changes you are targeting to make. Ask them to give you some input and let them know that you are looking for encouragement. Based on your personality type, you will desire encouragement more or less than others. It can be extremely helpful.

If you don't have people around you that you trust, and even if you do, look to find an example of the success you want to achieve and observe it. Whether it is a person or a business model, you can gain much from becoming an audience yourself. Study the success of others. Imagine the world you want.

Beyond that, here are some tips about working with an audience while taking new steps or using new skills in front of an audience. Let these take stress off you.

Regarding presentation skills or acting skills, the audience wants you to succeed. This is because if the speaker is uncomfortable, the audience will feel uncomfortable too. Few people enjoy that so you can assume that the vast majority of them want you to succeed.

Your audience assumes you know what you're doing. They expect it is why you are doing it.

Your audience hopes that you have the answers they are looking for.

About making mistakes. Most of the time, only you know if you made a mistake. So don't highlight it. If it is so obvious that you made a mistake, make a simple comment and move on.

As a corporate trainer I gained freedom the day I realized that the audience didn't know my next sentence or my next slide. In this case, what they didn't know couldn't hurt me.

Pausing to check notes is fine and quite normal for most presentations.

Eye contact. Here are a few tips that can help you for public speaking or in small groups.

Focus on your allies in the room.

If you're in a room full of people, you can look above their eyes to a spot in the back of the room. This can help you stay focused on your topic or content.

If you notice yourself constantly wanting to focus on the person who has the opinion you are most concerned with, start to choose other people to look at, on purpose.

When in a small group, be sure to share eye contact with everyone. In a large group, share it across the room and to every corner.

10

Encourage Yourself

Most people are too hard on themselves when it comes to change. Unfortunately, many people grew up in a zone filled with criticism or even trauma and loss. If that was your story, then becoming your own best encourager will be a critical shift to make.

If you don't become a good friend to yourself, it is extremely likely you will not remain successful long term. We can only bully or plead ourselves into high performance for so long.

I've seen people do it but they either crash eventually in their career or relationships or even seem to make themselves sick.

You simply MUST become patient and kind to yourself. This way of behaving with yourself must become a comfort zone of its own or most likely you will end up back in your original comfort zones, or worse, you will succumb to negative predictions said over and over about you.

If that scares you, it should. It may be a rare time that fear can help.

Promise yourself that you will make peace with yourself and take responsibility for fighting for you.

The "universe" is not against you. The God of the bible is for you. Some people are for you and some may be against you. What matters once you accept these other statements is, are you for you?

The negative comfort zones built by the unfortunate mind of those who grew up under criticism often have a very hard time not making excuses and finding someone to blame. Sometimes that someone is self.

Blaming yourself can lead to self-criticism and self-hatred. Words like, "I'm so stupid. I'll never get this right. I don't know why I even try..." need to become off limits. Self-criticism is not a motivator; it is a thief.

When you make mistakes, and you will, you need to be a patient friend to yourself. You need to be a kind friend to yourself. You need to be a forgiving and encouraging friend to yourself.

My last story. During a time in my life when I was stuck, I got a picture in my mind that really helped me change in this area. It was somewhat of a breakthrough. It was like a little movie scene about how I had no choice but to make friends with myself.

I saw myself sitting in a chair at a small round table in a plain room. My arms were folded, and the heels of my shoes were dug into the floor. I was angry, deeply hurt and determined. Then a second person, who was also me, walked into the room and saw myself sitting at the table. The me that walked in was working on a plan to accomplish something and was expecting that the seated Lenora would help. But it was very clear that she did not like me. The me in the chair looked at the me with a plan. With unquestionable determination and with fierce eyes, she slowly and deliberately said "I will not help you." She knew she was the key to success but she didn't care about the success she cared about the relationship. She'd had enough and she meant it.

I saw that the me with a plan was in trouble. At the time, the Lenora with a plan only cared about getting what she wanted. She was not nice to the Lenora sitting in the chair, she had never had to be. At the time, she would have moved on without the seated self but she knew inside that it was impossible. The Lenora with a plan had only one choice, to fail or to stop and reconcile with the Lenora who was the heart of all the work. She needed to make friends with the Lenora who had always helped in the past and used to be excited about it, but she had become so offended by the way that Lenora with a plan treated her, bullied her, criticized her and never thanked her or appreciated or played with her, that she quit. The seated Lenora was the amazingly kind Lenora but she wasn't the weak one, she was the one with all the power. The standing one was the driven one, good for ideas and parts of the strategies.

From that split second scene, I learned what the following famous saying meant: "Guard your heart with all diligence for out of it come the issues of life." Proverbs 4:23.

The Lenora with the plan represented my mind. The Lenora in the chair represented my heart. The heart is known to be the seat of our affections. The word affections originally included all of what we have considered positive and negative passions or emotions, not just romantic ones.

Does this example help you? I hope so because the image and the understanding brought the beginning of a change in the way I treated myself and shut down my own heart. I knew I had to become a real friend to myself if I wanted any power for success. I had no option but to change my way and reconcile with myself if I wanted to move forward. I could no longer remain comfortable treating myself like a slave. Thankfully, I changed directions by changing my actions. My mind and my heart became friends again.

Your self-talk and self-treatment will enable either long-term success or long-term failure. I really hope you will love and respect who you are and demonstrate it by new daily actions. Walk and talk it out.

Please answer the following questions.

On a scale of 1 to 10 do you like yourself? Ten equals you have great honor for yourself. ____

On a scale of 1 to 10 do you treat yourself well? Ten equals great patience and kindness with no record of wrongs. ____

If your numbers are lower than 7 will you make changing this comfort zone your top priority?

If your numbers are 7 or 8, keep growing because we struggle with how we treat others when deep down we don't, by visible action, care for ourselves.

11

Conclusion

Y ou chose this book because you want more for yourself. Most people do but too many don't realize that their current comfort zones and the resulting habits are what sabotage even the attempts for success.

If you grew up with physical or emotional abuse, you suffered trauma and both tangible and intangible losses. We all have suffered from various kinds of loss, but some have faced more loss than others. I highly recommend gaining additional information and support on grief recovery if you find that you struggle with depression and anxiety. Beyond painful beliefs, the grief of loss can become a root of fear and a weight you carry unnecessarily if you don't know how to take a practical path to recovery. I highly recommend the Grief Recovery Method and the Grief Recovery Handbook for anyone. There is a link to a podcast episode with the CEO, Cole James in the resource section. Bouldercrest.org is another resource I recommend for veterans and first responders. Information and a podcast interview link will be in the resource section. One on one coaching or counseling may also be a brilliant tool for breakthrough support or seasons of change.

You now have some understanding about how comfort zones are created in the subconscious mind and why they are so effective at keeping people from making significant changes in their lives.

Remember your brain is just trying to protect you though it can be quite wrong. Through questions and conversations, you can discover what some of the boundaries of your current zones are so that you can disarm the mental thoughts, cross those zones and exchange them for bigger and better comfort zones.

Some of your most powerful tools are your imagination, your words, and the actions you practice consistently. Use these tools for your success and stop their use against you.

Whenever possible, practice in the new zone and repeat until you get comfortable there.

Become your own best partner and encourager. Applaud yourself for every step you take. Like a baby's first steps, be inspired and excited about the new learning happening. Falling is just part of the process. Focus on the courage to take steps.

When you're taking new steps, tell yourself that you're not scared, you're excited. Sometimes that will make you laugh, often it really works!

Plan to live long term in your new zones and whenever you want to, read this book again and begin imagining your next new comfort zone. **You have the tools and you are completely worth the journey!**

Finally, it was an honor to write for you. Your potential is far beyond your awareness. I imagine you'll take the steps to get comfortable reaching it.

Of course, I would greatly appreciate a positive review from you on amazon.com. This will help more people discover the power of comfort zones and how to exchange them. Will you do that right now?

I'll imagine you will. Thank you in advance!

12

Resources

The Fourth Dimension: Combined. . . by Yonggi Cho, Dr. David. (n.d.). https://www.amazon.com/Fourth-Dimension-David-Yonggi-Cho/dp/1610369998dictionary

Home. (n.d.). The Grief Recovery Method. https://www.griefrecovery method.com/

Boulder Crest Foundation - the Home of Posttraumatic Growth (PTG). (2023, October 19). Boulder Crest Foundation. https://bouldercrest.org/

Facing losses in healthy ways - back to one. (n.d.). Buzzsprout. https://www.buzzsprout.com/1143872/10309979

From PTSD to post traumatic growth - E10 - Back to one. (n.d.). Buzzsprout. https://www.buzzsprout.com/1143872/5043194

The people code and making relationships work E29 - Back to one. (n.d.). Buzzsprout. https://www.buzzsprout.com/1143872/8280070

About the Author

Lenora Turner has performed in front of thousands as a theatrical comic host, has trained thousands of leaders across the US and multiple countries, has written articles and interviewed top executives globally. As an author, coach, podcast host and former Director at a Fortune 500 company for youth and veterans, Lenora offers amazing perspective and practical strategies for personal and professional goals. With a passion for individual and team success, Lenora is a powerful keynote speaker that inspires results.

You can connect with me on:
- https://3psinapod.buzzsprout.com
- https://www.linkedin.com/in/lenora-d

Made in the USA
Las Vegas, NV
07 March 2024